For Nolan

"Life is more fun if you play games."
— Roald Dahl

Let's Play

Rock, Paper, Scissors

A playfully connecting, social, communication book game.

Robert Jason Grant

AutPlay® Publishing

Let's Play Rock, Paper, Scissors: A Playfully Connecting, Social, Communication Book Game.

©2016 Robert Jason Grant Ed.D
Springfield, Missouri: AutPlay® Publishing
A Robert Jason Grant Ed.D Product

All rights reserved. No part of this book may be reproduced, stored in a retrieval system, or transmitted, in any form or by any means, electronic, mechanical, photo copying, microfilming, recording, or otherwise, without written permission of the author.

Instructions, game pages, and any other parts of this book may be reproduced only within the confines of the use with clients. This limited permission does not grant other rights, nor does it give permission for commercial, resale, syndication, or any other use not contained above. Any other use, or reproduction, is a violation of international laws and is forbidden without express written permission from the author.

ISBN: 978-0-9882718-7-6

All Images Provided By ClipArtLord.com

Correspondence regarding this book:
Robert Jason Grant Ed.D/AutPlay Publishing
DrGrant@robertjasongrant.com
info@autplaytherapy.com
www.robertjasongrant.com
www.autplaytherapy.com

A Bit About This Book Game

Let's Play Rock, Paper, Scissors is a creatively designed book game. Therapists, school counselors, parents, and other professionals working with children and adolescents can utilize this book to address a variety of issues. *Let's Play Rock, Paper, Scissors* follows a psychoeducational model incorporating elements of cognitive behavioral therapy, play therapy, and relationship development approaches. This book game addresses a plethora of skills children and adolescents may need to improve upon including:

- Improvement in communication ability
- Social skill development
- Improvement in engagement and attachment skills
- Addressing sensory and regulation challenges
- Improvement in play skills
- Relationship development

Professionals and parents can also use *Let's Play Rock, Paper, Scissors* as a rapport building tool and assessment instrument to learn more about the child or adolescent. It functions as a useful resource for both individual and family therapy. As a structured intervention, *Let's Play Rock, Paper, Scissors* can be incorporated into treatment planning to help address the above listed issues.

Each page of this book begins with one of six brief, engaging, connection activities. The connection activities are: the rock, paper, scissor hand game, thumb wrestle, staring game (don't blink), patty cake categories, freeze (don't move), and feelings face off. Whoever wins the activity chooses from a list of five interactive options. The winner decides what he or she will do, and what the other person playing the game will do. The five interactive options are: answer the question, top 3, what if, complete the sentence, and do this. Players should start on the first page of play and continue through the end of the book game. There are 30 game play pages. *Let's Play Rock, Paper, Scissors* book game can be played repeatedly, going through the book game multiple times with difficult interactive options chosen to complete.

Professionals and parents can have a fun and engaging experience with children and adolescents through the connection activities, and can ask follow up questions and role model when participating in the interactive options. Children and adolescents who will benefit from this game book include: those struggling with communication and social skills, those struggling with emotion regulation and engagement, and those with a diagnosis of ADHD, autism spectrum disorder, sensory processing struggles, and related disorders.

Instructions

How to Play:

Let's Play Rock, Paper, Scissors is designed for two players but may be adapted for up to four players. Players start with the first play page. The players complete a connection activity (see below). Whoever wins the connection activity then chooses what both players will do from among the five interactive options listed on the page. The five interactive options on each page are: 1) Answer the question, 2) Say your top three, 3) What if, 4) Complete the sentence, and 5) Do this. Once the interactive options have been completed, the players move to the next page following the same instructions. There are 30 total game pages to complete. *Let's Play Rock, Paper, Scissors* can be played repeatedly with new interactive options chosen each time.

The Six Connection Activities:

1. Rock Paper Scissors
   A hand game played between two people, in which each player on the count of three simultaneously forms one of

three shapes with an outstretched hand. These shapes are "rock" (a simple fist), "paper" (a flat hand), and "scissors" (a fist with the index and middle fingers together forming a V). The game has three possible outcomes other than a tie: a player who decides to play rock will beat another player who has chosen scissors ("rock crushes scissors") but will lose to one who has played paper ("paper covers rock"); a play of paper will lose to a play of scissors ("scissors cut paper"). If both players choose the same shape, the game is tied and is replayed to break the tie. The game can be played once or best out of three.

2. Thumb Wrestle
In this game, two players lock fingers with one hand. They lay their thumbs on top of their closed fist. On the count of three each person taps their thumb on alternating sides of their fists looking for the opportunity to pin their opponent's thumb under their own. The first person to pin the other person's thumb is the winner.

3. Staring Game (don't blink)
This is a staring contest where two people stare at each other making eye contact until one person blinks or looks away. The first person to blink or look away loses the contest.

4. Patty Cake Categories
A simple hand clapping game played with two people, hands are clapped in a standard crisscross motion with each other in a comfortable rhythm. In Patty Cake Categories, an additional instruction is added to the simple hand clapping game. While the players are hand clapping, they must keep naming things from a pre-

chosen category such as emotions, animals, fruits, or sports (the adult and child can decide together what category they want to use before the game begins). There can be no repeats and once someone is unable to think of anything to say or repeats what has already been said, the game is over. The first person to repeat something that has already been said, or cannot think of anything to say, loses the game.

5. Freeze (don't move)
   Players must freeze their whole body and face. Players must remain frozen until one of the players moves, whoever moves first loses the game.

6. Feelings Face Off
   One player begins by naming an emotion. The next player then names a different emotion. Play moves back and forth with each player naming a different emotion until one player repeats an emotion that has already been said or cannot think of anything to say. The first person to repeat an emotion or cannot think of anything to say loses the game. This game can also be played using paper and taking turns writing the emotions down.

The six connection activities are designed to be fun and playful. Therapists and parents should make this part of the game fun and enjoyable for the child or adolescent. These activities are simple and require no props, yet they create an engagement between the adult and child and promote attachment and social interaction. If the professional or parent are able to win every game, the professional or parent should let the child or adolescent win some of the games so that the child or adolescent has the opportunity to choose some of the interactive options. This book game works best when both the adult and the child win some of the connection games, and thus each can contribute to choosing some of the interactive options.

The five interactive options vary from questions to completing tasks. These interactive options provide opportunity to work on social skill development, engaging with another person, improving communication skills, practicing sensory processing activities, improving emotional regulation and awareness, strengthening rapport and relationship, gathering assessment information, and simply having fun!

Let's Play

Rock, Paper, Scissors

(Winner chooses who does what below)

Answer the Question

Who is the funniest person in your family?

Say Your Top 3

Worst foods

What If

Your best friend moved in with you?

Complete the Sentence

I am calm when…

Do This

Run in place for 5 seconds

Let's Play

Thumb Wrestle

(Winner chooses who does what below)

Answer the Question

Have you ever felt uncomfortable around other kids?

Say Your Top 3

Favorite family members

What If

You had to wear a uniform everyday?

Complete the Sentence

One day I will…

Do This

Laugh

Let's Play

Staring Game (don't blink)

(Winner chooses who does what below)

Answer the Question

Have you ever helped someone else?

Say Your Top 3

Fun places to go

What If

You lived by yourself?

Complete the Sentence

When I am mad I…

Do This

Stand up and touch your fingers to your toes

Let's Play

Patty Cake Categories

(Winner chooses who does what below)

Answer the Question

What is a favorite trip you have been on?

Say Your Top 3

Things to do with your family

What If

You could only eat one food the rest of your life?

Complete the Sentence

School is…

Do This

Give someone a high five

Let's Play

Freeze (don't move)

(Winner chooses who does what below)

Answer the Question

Who is the weirdest person in your family?

Say Your Top 3

Wishes for your future

What If

You felt mad all the time?

Complete the Sentence

The worst thing that could happen is…

Do This

Count to ten slowly

Let's Play

Feelings Face Off

(Winner chooses who does what below)

Answer the Question

What are the names of your friends?

Say Your Top 3

Things that make you feel happy

What If

Someone gave you $100?

Complete the Sentence

My best quality is…

Do This

Act like you're playing a sport

Let's Play

Rock, Paper, Scissors

(Winner chooses who does what below)

Answer the Question

What is your favorite toy or game?

Say Your Top 3

Holidays

What If

You felt sad all the time?

Complete the Sentence

Dear parents…

Do This

Give yourself a body hug

Let's Play

Thumb Wrestle

(Winner chooses who does what below)

Answer the Question

How do you like to play?

Say Your Top 3

Restaurants

What If

A new kid at school wanted to sit by you at lunch?

Complete the Sentence

I wish I could…

Do This

Make a confused face

Let's Play

Staring Game (don't blink)

(Winner chooses who does what below)

Answer the Question

When do you feel happy?

Say Your Top 3

Worst chores

What If

You had to do chores all day long?

Complete the Sentence

Teachers are…

Do This

Pretend you are punching a punching bag

Let's Play

Patty Cake Categories

(Winner chooses who does what below)

Answer the Question

How would you change your family?

Say Your Top 3

Favorite school subjects

What If

You never went to school?

Complete the Sentence

Bullies are…

Do This

Walk in slow motion around the room

Let's Play

Freeze (don't move)

(Winner chooses who does what below)

Answer the Question

When do you feel calm?

Say Your Top 3

Things you wish you had

What If

Every kid at school wanted to be your friend?

Complete the Sentence

People think I am…

Do This

Jump as high as you can

Let's Play

Feelings Face Off

(Winner chooses who does what below)

Answer the Question

When do you feel worried?

Say Your Top 3

Teachers

What If

You didn't have parents?

Complete the Sentence

My safe place is…

Do This

Pretend like you're playing the drums

Let's Play

Rock, Paper, Scissors

(Winner chooses who does what below)

Answer the Question

Do you like school?

Say Your Top 3

Things someone can do if they are bullied

What If

You could do whatever you wanted?

Complete the Sentence

My greatest accomplishment is…

Do This

Spin around 3 times

Let's Play

Thumb Wrestle

(Winner chooses who does what below)

Answer the Question

When do you feel confident?

Say Your Top 3

Scary things

What If

Your family moved to another state?

Complete the Sentence

I think about…

Do This

Act like an animal

Let's Play

Staring Game (don't blink)

(Winner chooses who does what below)

Answer the Question

When was a time you felt sorry?

Say Your Top 3

Favorite things about school

What If

Other kids asked you to play with them?

Complete the Sentence

Being happy means…

Do This

Pretend you are an airplane flying around the room

Let's Play

Patty Cake Categories

(Winner chooses who does what below)

Answer the Question

How would you change yourself?

Say Your Top 3

Toys

What If

You were the most popular kid in school?

Complete the Sentence

I am sad when…

Do This

Tell a joke

Let's Play

Freeze (don't move)

(Winner chooses who does what below)

Answer the Question

Have you ever been bullied?

Say Your Top 3

Things that make you mad

What If

You became a professional athlete?

Complete the Sentence

I wish my parents would…

Do This

Act like you are swimming

Let's Play

Feelings Face Off

(Winner chooses who does what below)

Answer the Question

What is one of your favorite things to do?

Say Your Top 3

Feelings

What If

School lasted all year long?

Complete the Sentence

I am scared of…

Do This

Walk backwards around the room

Let's Play

Rock, Paper, Scissors

(Winner chooses who does what below)

Answer the Question

Do you think kids should participate in groups or clubs?

Say Your Top 3

Things that make you feel calm

What If

Someone designed a video game based on your life?

Complete the Sentence

Dear Dad...

Do This

Take 3 deep breaths

Let's Play

Thumb Wrestle

(Winner chooses who does what below)

Answer the Question

What is the worst quality a person can have?

Say Your Top 3

Sports

What If

Someone wrote a book about your family?

Complete the Sentence

People don't like it when I…

Do This

Hop on one foot around the room

Let's Play

Staring Game (don't blink)

(Winner chooses who does what below)

Answer the Question

What do you think is the best quality a person can have?

Say Your Top 3

Ways kids get bullied

What If

Everyone in school was invited to a party except you?

Complete the Sentence

When I play I…

Do This

Make an angry face

Let's Play

Patty Cake Categories

(Winner chooses who does what below)

Answer the Question

Who in your family is most like you?

Say Your Top 3

Favorite video or computer games

What If

You had to stay in your room for 3 days?

Complete the Sentence

I am good at…

Do This

Act like you are playing a video game

Let's Play

Freeze (don't move)

(Winner chooses who does what below)

Answer the Question

What are some reasons that kids should attend school?

Say Your Top 3

People you would like to be friends with

What If

Your favorite toy got destroyed?

Complete the Sentence

I feel confused when…

Do This

Pretend like you are crawling through a cave

Let's Play

Feelings Face Off

(Winner chooses who does what below)

Answer the Question

What is something you like to do with other kids?

Say Your Top 3

Things that make you nervous

What If

You had to act in a play?

Complete the Sentence

My parents are…

Do This

Make a silly face

Let's Play

Rock, Paper, Scissors

(Winner chooses who does what below)

Answer the Question

What is the hardest part about being in school?

Say Your Top 3

Bad memories

What If

Everyone you knew had a party for you?

Complete the Sentence

Dear Mom…

Do This

Create a special handshake

Let's Play

Thumb Wrestle

(Winner chooses who does what below)

Answer the Question

Has there been a time you have felt rejected or left out?

Say Your Top 3

Movies or TV shows

What If

There were no more computers?

Complete the Sentence

Friends are…

Do This

5 jumping jacks

Let's Play

Staring Game (don't blink)

(Winner chooses who does what below)

Answer the Question

How would you describe yourself?

Say Your Top 3

Things about your home

What If

You lost all your hair?

Complete the Sentence

I don't like…

Do This

Act like you are blowing up a balloon

Let's Play

Patty Cake Categories

(Winner chooses who does what below)

Answer the Question

What is something you have done to be a good friend?

Say Your Top 3

Musical Instruments

What If

Your eyes changed color?

Complete the Sentence

When I get worried I…

Do This

Twist your body like a pretzel

Let's Play

Freeze (don't move)

(Winner chooses who does what below)

Answer the Question

How would you describe your school?

Say Your Top 3

Best things about you

What If

Some tried to scare you?

Complete the Sentence

Everyone in my family…

Do This

Act like you are climbing a tree

Let's Play

Feelings Face Off

(Winner chooses who does what below)

Answer the Question

When you get upset, what do you do?

Say Your Top 3

Favorite animals

What If

There were no rules?

Complete the Sentence

When I am an adult I will…

Do This

Pretend like you are relaxing

Let's Play Again!

About Dr. Robert Jason Grant

Dr. Grant is a Licensed Professional Counselor, National Certified Counselor, Registered Play Therapist Supervisor, and Certified Autism Specialist. Dr. Grant completed his education from Missouri State University receiving a B.S. in Psychology and M.S. in Counseling. Dr. Grant further received his doctorate degree in Education from the University of Missouri-Columbia.

Dr. Grant operates a private practice mental health clinic in Southwest Missouri where he specializes in play therapy techniques with children, adolescents, adults, and families. Dr. Grant also specializes in working with Autism Spectrum Disorder, Neurodevelopmetnal Disorders, and Developmental Disabilities and is the creator of AutPlay® Therapy, an Autism treatment using play therapy, behavioral therapy, and relationship development approaches.

Dr. Grant has authored several publications and has written five books about play therapy, Autism, and ADHD including *AutPlay therapy for children and adolescents on the autism spectrum: a behavioral play-based approach*. He is a professional board member for Stars for Autism and Infinity Academy and is a contributing writer for the *Missouri Autism Report*. Dr. Grant conducts various presentations and workshops on topics such as play therapy and Autism. Dr. Grant has conducted trainings and workshops throughout the United States and has presented at various area and national conferences including the American Counseling Association, the American Mental Health Counselors Association, and the Association for Play Therapy.

Learn more about Dr. Grant and inquire about the trainings, products, and therapy he offers at www.robertjasongrant.com and www.autplaytherapy.com. You may also connect with Dr. Grant though Facebook, Twitter, LinkedIn, and Pinterest via Robert Jason Grant Ed.D and AutPlay Therapy.

Additional Products by Dr. Robert Jason Grant

- *The Autism Spectrum Disorder Workbook for Children*
- *The Autism Spectrum Disorder Workbook for Teens*
- *AutPlay® Therapy for Children and Adolescents on the Autism Spectrum: A Behavioral Play-Based Approach*
- *Play-Based Interventions for Autism Spectrum Disorder and Other Developmental Disabilities*
- *Understanding Sensory Processing: A Workbook for Children and Teens*

www.robertjasongrant.com
www.autplaytherapy.com

Made in the USA
Coppell, TX
14 December 2019